FISHING

Graham Beehag

Weigl

www.weigl.com

Published by Weigl Educational Publishers Limited
6325 – 10 Street SE
Calgary, Alberta, Canada
T2H 2Z9
Web site: www.weigl.com

Library and Archives Canada Cataloguing in Publication

Beehag, Graham
     Fishing / Graham Beehag.

(Canadian industries series)
Includes index.
ISBN 1-55388-226-1 (bound)
ISBN 1-55388-227-X (pbk.)

     1. Fisheries--Canada--Juvenile literature. 2. Fisheries--Economic aspects--Canada--Juvenile literature. 3. Fisheries--Canada--History-- Juvenile literature. I. Title. II. Series: Canadian industries (Calgary, Alta.)

SH223.B45 2007   j338.3'7270971   C2006-902500-2

Printed in Canada
1 2 3 4 5 6 7 8 9 0 10 09 08 07 06

All of the internet URLs given in the book were valid at the time of publication. However, due to the dynamic nature of the internet, some addresses may have changed, or sites may have ceased to exist since publication. While the author and publisher regret any inconvenience this may cause readers, no responsibility for any such changes can be accepted by either the author or the publisher.

Project Coordinator: Heather Kissock
Designer: Warren Clark

We gratefully acknowledge the financial support of the Government of Canada through the Book Publishing Industry Development Program (BPIDP) for our publishing activities.

Credits: Every reasonable effort has been made to trace ownership and to obtain permission to reprint copyright material. The publishers would be pleased to have any errors or omissions brought to their attention so that they may be corrected in subsequent printings.
Photo courtesy of Ihor Szulhan: page 10.

Contents

Overview 4

Canadian Fishing 6

Fishing in Canada 8

Fishing a Nation 10

Then and Now 12

Aquaculture 14

Seal Hunting 16

Careers in Fishing 18

Facing the Issues 20

Fishing in the World 22

Fishing Around the World 24

Charting Fishing in the World 26

Supplying the Demand 28

From Canada to the World ...30

Fishing Science 32

Fishing's Impact on Canadians 34

Helping Others 36

Looking to the Future 38

Timeline of Fishing Events ...40

Research Activity 42

Fish Recipe 43

What Do You Know? 44

Further Research 46

Glossary 47

Index 48

Overview

From its land to its people, Canada is a diverse country. This diversity lends itself to a range of industries. Major industries in Canada include agriculture, energy, fishing, forestry, mining, and **manufacturing**. Each of these industries require people with various skills. As a result, Canadians can work in almost any field they like without leaving the country. People from other countries view Canada as a land of opportunity as well. Many come to Canada to find work, to create businesses, or to otherwise contribute to the economic landscape.

Canada's industries have global impact. The country's natural resources are shipped both raw and as manufactured products to many parts of the world. Sometimes, they are sold to other countries. On other occasions, they are sent for humanitarian

Agriculture

Agriculture, or farming, is an industry that uses the land to grow crops and raise animals for food and other products. Canadian crops include grains, such as wheat, barley, and canola, as well as fruits and vegetables. Cattle, sheep, and swine are just some of the animals raised on Canada's farms.

Energy

Energy provides the electricity that lights rooms, the gas that makes cars and trucks run, and the oil that heats buildings. It comes from natural resources such as water, natural gas, petroleum, coal, and uranium. Due to the abundance of these resources, Canada is a world leader in energy production.

Fishing

With 202,080 kilometres of coastline, Canada has access to more fish and shellfish than most other countries. Salmon, cod, and sole are just some of the fish caught off Canada's coasts. Shellfish caught in Canada's waters include lobster and shrimp. Fish farms, in which fish are raised and harvested like farm animals, also contribute to the fishing industry in Canada.

purposes, in order to help countries that have an urgent need for materials. Canadian products are known worldwide for their quality. In order to maintain and improve this quality, Canadians are constantly developing and implementing new technologies and methods, all the while keeping an eye on the impact these technologies have on people and the environment.

Canadians can work in almost any field they like without leaving the country.

Forestry

Forests cover about 40 percent of Canada's land surface, and approximately 245 million hectares of these forests are timber-productive. This means that the trees in these areas can be used to manufacture other products. Spruce, pine, cedar, and fir are all timber-productive trees found in Canada's forests.

Mining

Minerals of all kinds are found deep inside Canada's land. These minerals have a range of uses. Once it is mined from the ground, Canada's zinc is used in sunscreen. Its sand and gravel are used to build houses and roads. Its gold and diamonds are used to make jewelry. Other minerals mined in Canada include copper, potash, and nickel.

Manufacturing

Canada uses its natural resources to create a variety of products. At pulp and paper mills, trees are used to make paper. Nickel is used to create stainless steel for eating utensils. Besides sunscreen, zinc is also used to create the galvanized steel used in the construction of buildings, aircraft parts, and telecommunication equipment.

Canadian Fishing

Fishing is an industry of significant importance for Canada, a country surrounded by three major oceans and home to five Great Lakes. Canada has the world's largest coastline (244,000 kilometres) which, if stretched out in a continuous line, would circle the equator more than six times. With two million lakes and rivers, Canada also has the largest freshwater system in the world. It has 16 percent of the entire area of freshwater on the planet.

Canada exports more than 75 percent of its fishing and seafood production all over the world.

It is no surprise that fishing is a major national pastime, both as a sport and as a means of making money. In 2000, more than 3.6 million adults went recreational fishing; almost 233 million fish were caught during this time. Many of the seven million people who live along this coastline depend on the ocean's resources to make a living.

The Canadian commercial fishing industry is one of the world's most valuable, bringing in more than $5 billion yearly and providing more than 130,000

Trawlers carry large catches of fish, while buoys mark the locations of fishing nets and traps.

Biologists sometimes work with hatcheries to help raise fish such as salmon.

jobs to people in 1,500 communities. Both the fishing and aquaculture industries operate in three broad regions across the country: Atlantic, Pacific, and freshwater.

Each year, more than one million tonnes of marine and freshwater fish and seafood are caught in Canada. Salmon, lobster, crab, shrimp, and scallops bring in the most revenue, with the bulk harvested in the Atlantic. The freshwater fishery brings in species such as lake trout, pickerel and yellow perch.

Canada **exports** more than 75 percent of its fishing and seafood production to more than 130 countries. The United States is the main importer of Canadian fish and seafood products, followed by China, Japan and the European Union. This trade is worth more than $5 billion a year in the Canadian economy.

In 2001, there were 23,360 commercial fishing vessels registered, and the value of Canada's fisheries came in at $2.14 billion. Related businesses in the ocean sector include transportation, coastal tourism, construction, engineering, and fish processing.

Aquaculture, the farming of fish and seafood, is a growing industry and now contributes a significant addition to the fishing industry, both in terms of production and jobs.

There are problems for Canadian fishing. The amount of cod in the oceans that surround Canada's coastline has declined dramatically in recent years. This is due mainly to over-fishing by fleets of huge factory fishing fleets from all over the world. These fleets virtually destroyed the stocks in the Atlantic waters, so much so that a **moratorium** was imposed upon the fishing of cod more than 10 years ago. This is to give the fish stocks time to regenerate and become **sustainable** for future generations. The numbers of cod in the Atlantic are now increasing, but not as fast as was hoped. It will be some years before the stock has revived sufficiently to allow sustainable fishing to continue.

BUSINESS BITS

About seven million people live in coastal areas of Canada. Many rely on the ocean's resources and tourism to make their living.

Lobster, crab, and shrimp make up 67 percent of the value of all fish and shellfish harvested in Canada.

Fishing in Canada

Surrounded by the Arctic, Atlantic, and Pacific Oceans, Canada has some of the most productive fisheries in the world. The area of Canada's offshore waters is equal to 37 percent of the total landmass of the country. Inland there are huge areas of commercial and recreational fishing. More than 2 million freshwater lakes and rivers cover 7.6 percent of Canada's total land mass with water. The longest inland waterway is from the Gulf of St. Lawrence to Lake Superior.

THINK ABOUT IT ▼

This map shows the areas where the different species of sea life are caught in Canada. How often do you eat fish or seafood? What is your favourite fish? Does it come from the sea or fresh water? Do you eat more fish that come from the oceans, or more from the freshwater fisheries?

Pacific Salmon

Atlantic Cod

Lobster

Flounder and Sole

Pacific Halibut

GREENLAND

Baffin Bay

Nunavut

Iqaluit

Saskatchewan

Manitoba

Hudson Bay

Newfoundland

St. John's

L. Winnipeg

Q u e b e c

Prince Edward Island

O n t a r i o

New Brunswick

Charlottetown

Regina

Winnipeg

Fredericton

Nova Scotia

Halifax

Lake Superior

Quebec

Montreal

Ottawa

Lake Huron

Lake Michigan

Lake Ontario

Toronto

Lake Erie

Fishing a Nation

The Canadian fishing industry first began when Jacques Cartier sailed into the Gulf of St. Lawrence in 1534. Based along the Atlantic Coast, the French fishery that developed over the next 200 years was extremely successful due to religious reasons. At the time, most of Europe was Roman Catholic and followed a number of rules and rituals, including one that forbade them to eat meat on Fridays. Because they did not consider fish to be meat, their demand for it was increased, and the French saw it as a profitable way to satisfy their palates as well as their religious beliefs.

Lobster fishermen once used dories to lay traps. Later, they used outboard engines. Now, some boats have GPS, radar, and sonar equipment.

European fishers originally used the waters surrounding Newfoundland as a cod fishery. It was a useful and increasingly important addition to fisheries carried on in European waters.

From the early 16th century, fishing ships sailed to Newfoundland from France, Spain and Portugal each spring, returning in the fall with their catch of salted codfish. In the 17th century, the Spanish and Portuguese fishing fleets declined, and fishing ships from England took their place.

In the late 1700s, Americans began controlling the fishing industry, with special emphasis on the mackerel fish. As these fish began to decline, so did the number of fishers, who gradually returned to their own coasts.

Trading between French and English merchants and the planters and settlers who

made Newfoundland their home grew well into the 1800s. By this time, the fishery was in the control of the settlers. The English migratory fishery had dwindled, and eventually the colonial society it had created in Newfoundland took over. The fisheries remained economically important to both France and England, and French fishing ships continued to fish there into the 20th century.

The number of people who were involved in Canada's fishing industry increased during the latter part of the 19th century and early 1900s. Due to **industrialization**, those numbers soon dropped.

> From the early 16th century, fishing ships sailed to Newfoundland from France, Spain and Portugal each spring.

One major effect of industrialization came about as the sail was gradually replaced by the motor engine, allowing boats to be more easily maneuvered and for a smaller number of crew to do the work. As new technology, such as refrigeration, was developed, this second effect of industrialization meant processing techniques were quicker and more efficient, thereby needing less people to do it. As factories began to be built in the larger cities, fewer fishers were choosing to stay behind to do their traditional jobs. During the **Great Depression**, many of those who lost their jobs returned to fishing but left it behind again to join the armed forces during World War II.

After the war, people soon returned to the fishing industry, and production increased steadily until the stock of cod fell drastically in the late 1980s and early 1990s. The inshore fisheries were not badly affected by the decline of cod stocks, and the labour force of around 5,000 people has continued to grow steadily.

Jacques Cartier

In 1534, Jacques Cartier, an explorer, sailed from St. Malo in northern France to look for a route to Asia. During this search, he explored what later became known as Newfoundland, the Magdalen Islands, Prince Edward Island, and the Gaspé Peninsula.

The king of France, François I, sent Cartier back to Canada on a second voyage in 1535, with three ships and 110 men to explore further.

Cartier's third voyage was not just a voyage of exploration. The king wanted Cartier to help start a new colony. He left France in 1541 with five ships and 1,500 people. The winter that year was very hard in Canada, and they had many problems with poor food and **scurvy**. By June 1542, many of the settlers had died. Cartier returned to France with the survivors.

The cod and whales that Cartier reported when he returned to France were significant, and whalers who sailed to Labrador and Newfoundland found that they could harpoon enough whales to become rich in a single trip.

Then and Now

Fishing has always been a hard and hazardous occupation. In the early days of Canadian fishing, men went out in boats that had only the most basic equipment. Over time, technology and science has helped modern fishers to fish in more safety.

THEN

THEN

Safety at Sea

The concept of safety in the fishing industry is a relatively new one, as it was not a major concern in the early days. Lifejackets and other safety equipment did not exist, even though many fishers could not even swim. Today, attitudes and technology have changed to make the work of a fisher far less perilous than it used to be. Crew members can now wear special buoyant worksuits that are waterproof with a lining of buoyant foam material. This material gives flotation and provides some protection from the cold should the fisher fall into the water.

NOW

Finding the Way

Before World War II, navigational technology remained at a very simple level in the fishing industry. Basic tools, such as **sextants**, and compasses, combined with memory and instinct often came in handy. Navigation using these simple methods was possible in clear weather, but it often became much more difficult in foggy or stormy conditions.

The most significant advances in navigational technology were made during and after World War II. Radio detection and ranging systems were independently developed by both Great Britain and the United States, who also created position-fixing systems to give accurate location information on boats. In 1973, the U.S. Department of Defence developed the Global Positioning System (GPS), which many boats use today for more precise navigation.

NOW

THEN

THEN

Catching the Fish

Nets have been used to catch fish for thousands of years. There are many different shapes and sizes of net depending on what type of fish is being caught and where they are located. Until the introduction of powered hauling rigs on trawlers, the catch was hauled in by the fisher. This is a tough and dangerous procedure. Huge **supertrawlers** of the developed nations use massive nets that are up to 0.4 kilometres wide across the ocean floor.

Processing the Catch

Salting used to be the only way to keep fish from spoiling. After being cleaned and washed, the fish were packed into large barrels of salt. The fish were then dried in the Sun or in kilns. Fish canning was once carried out by plants spread around the coast, but over time, many of the smaller canning factories have shut down. Modern fish processing plants not only clean and fillet the fish, they also produce fish and seafood products that may be dipped in a seasoning, covered with a sauce, or flaked and shaped into serving portions, before being frozen and packaged ready for the grocery stores.

NOW

NOW

Aquaculture

The farming of fish and shellfish for food is referred to as aquaculture. As the demand for fish and seafood increases, the aquaculture industry has become an important source of supply. The aquaculture industry offers new prosperity for residents of **rural** and coastal communities who have suffered in the decline of traditional coastal and offshore fishing.

Although it is a relatively new industry, aquaculture has grown at a steady pace of 20 percent each year since 1986. It is found in every province and territory in Canada, including 16 Aboriginal communities. The key products include farmed salmon, trout, Arctic char, blue mussels and oysters.

New species currently being developed include halibut and cod. If successful, cod grown in aquaculture can be used to help restore the depleted stocks in Atlantic waters. The top three provincial producers of aquaculture products are British Columbia, New Brunswick and Prince Edward Island.

Each year, the Canadian aquaculture industry provides more than 14,000 jobs both directly and indirectly and generates more than $1 billion in national economic activity. In 2001, the Canadian aquaculture industry produced about 22 percent of the total value of Canadian fish and seafood production, or about 152,000 tonnes.

Canada is one of the world's key suppliers of farmed salmon, and oysters that are cultured at Prince Edward Island are famous around the world.

In 2002, Canada ranked 22nd worldwide for aquaculture, though British Columbia was the fourth largest producer of farmed salmon in the world after Norway, Chile, and Great Britain.

> **Each year, the Canadian aquaculture industry provides more than 14,000 jobs.**

Oyster farming is part of the fast-growing aquaculture industry.

Profile

Bernard Martin

Jacques Cartier was amazed by the large number of fish his ships caught in the Grand Banks when he arrived in what is now Canada in 1534. He called the Grand Banks *terra dos baccalaos*, which in Portuguese means "land of cod."

The recent experiences of fishers, such as Bernard Martin, have been very different. In 1992, cod stocks in Canada's Atlantic waters experienced their lowest recorded levels. The Canadian government realized that the fishing industry could not sustain itself if these numbers were not increased. To protect cod, the government placed a moratorium on cod fishing in 1992. The moratorium put 30,000 fishers in Newfoundland and Labrador out of work, including Bernard Martin.

Martin, a fourth-generation fisher from Petty Harbour, a fishing community in Newfoundland, is a determined conservationist who encourages responsible management of Canada's fish stocks. Within the past 20 years, Martin has noticed a trend of over-fishing in other

In some parts of the world, over-fishing is a problem.

countries, so he travels around the world encouraging sustainable fishing. Helping him spread his conservation message are organizations such as

> **To protect cod, the government placed a moratorium on cod fishing in 1992.**

Oxfam, the Sierra Club, and Greenpeace.

The fishers of Petty Harbour saw that the numbers of fish were getting smaller and created the Petty Harbour/Maddox Cove Protected Fishing Area.

Martin believes that modern fish trawlers from both international and Canadian commercial fishing companies are a big problem for the fishing industry. In 1990, international fisheries took in 360,000 tonnes of cod in waters near the Grand Banks. Commercial Canadian fishing is also a problem for the inshore fishermen of communities. Many commercial boats use drag nets that kill creatures living on the ocean floor. Some commercial nets are made of plastic and do not biodegrade. If these nets are lost in the oceans, they can kill sea creatures. Martin suggests that avoiding plastic nets and returning to traditional fishing methods would help the fishing industry recover.

Martin hopes that one day, sustainable fishing will be a reality.

Atlantic Lobster

Lobster is harvested along the Atlantic coast of Canada. In fact, more than half of the world's supply is harvested on Canada's coasts. With sales totalling more than $1 billion each year, Atlantic lobster is Canada's top seafood export.

Most lobster fishing takes place within 15 kilometres of the shores of Newfoundland, New Brunswick, Nova Scotia, Prince Edward Island, and Quebec. However, eight vessels trap in the deep ocean off southwestern Nova Scotia. These vessels cannot come within 92 kilometres of the shoreline.

Over the years, there have been limited advances in the technology used to catch Atlantic cod. As in the past, lobster fishers drive small boats and lower traps into the water. Single traps are made from wood or plastic-coated metal, and they are baited to attract lobsters. Traps are lowered to the bottom of the ocean floor. A floating buoy marks the location of each trap. After a period of time, the traps are hauled to the surface. Although other methods are more efficient, they are less environmentally friendly and cause damage to the ocean floor. For this reason, single traps remain the most common lobster harvest method.

To maintain the integrity of the lobster harvest, certain conservation measures have been employed. In Canada, the Department of Fisheries and Oceans (DFO) regulates lobster catches and provides guidelines for their harvest. For example, the DFO has designated 41 lobster fishing areas along the

Lobsters are trapped off the coast of the Atlantic Province.

Atlantic lobster is Canada's top seafood export.

Atlantic coast. As well, each lobster fishing area can only be tapped at certain times of year. This helps ensure lobsters are protected during their summer moults so that hard-shelled, meaty lobsters are harvested for export. In addition to these conservation efforts, the DFO implements a many other guidelines, including limiting the number of trapping licenses available each year.

Most large lobsters are sold in fresh markets, while smaller lobsters are processed or frozen. Lobster processing plants face strict regulations and quality control management to ensure products meet health and safety standards.

Profile

AVC Lobster Science Centre

In July 2000, the Atlantic Veterinary College (AVC) on Prince Edward Island opened the (AVC) Lobster Science Centre. The centre is dedicated to researching lobster health on behalf in Atlantic Canada.

Located along the Atlantic coast, the Lobster Science Centre focusses on finding the causes of disease in lobsters, assessing the impact environmental stresses, finding vaccines for disease, and monitoring lobster health. The centre also compiles information for a web-based database that outlines processing, marketing and production information.

The Lobster Science Centre receives 45 percent of its funding from fishing companies, Aboriginal groups, and governments. The remaining funds are provided by the Atlantic Innovation Fund (AIF). Each of these partners oversees the operations of the centre and has a genuine interest in the lobster industry.

> "The centre is dedicated to researching lobster health on behalf of Atlantic Canada."

In order to ensure the sustainability of lobster as part of the Canadian seafood industry, the Lobster Science Centre has many goals. First, the centre seeks to increase lobster catches by researching handling, hold, and transportation measures. The centre also hopes to develop new technologies, create a skilled research team, and train highly knowledgeable professionals to work in Canada's lobster industry.

Traps are set and hauled on a cycle of about three days.

Careers in Fishing

Today's fishing industry is about more than catching fish. There is a wide range of jobs for men and women in fish processing, transport, and selling in international **markets**. Aquaculture is a growing industry that requires scientists and people with different skills from the traditional fishers.

Fishing Boat Captain

Duties: Plans and oversees the details of the fishing operation, from purchase of supplies and equipment, to selling the fish that is caught

Education: Two-year vocation-technical program offered by secondary schools and community colleges

Interests: Seamanship, marine safety, navigation, fishing gear technology

The fishing boat captain's ultimate goal is to catch, trap, and sell different kinds of marine life for a variety of uses. Captains plot the course of the vessel using electronic navigational equipment. They use radars to avoid possible obstacles, detect whether there is marine life nearby, and locate and analyze schools of fish. When the vessel returns to its port, the captain will coordinate the sale of the catch and ensure crew members get their fair share. More and more captains are using computers as a way to buy and sell fish over the internet. Sometimes captains will also use their **expertise** to guide tours for people who like to fish for sport or recreational purposes, taking out clients for hours or even days at a time.

Every fishing boat has a captain. Today, captains use many technologies, such as the telephone, to help them safely sail their boats.

Canadian Coast Guard Officer

Duties: Saves lives and protects the marine environment by responding to incidents of environmental pollution, supporting scientific surveys and helping fishing vessels and recreational boaters in distress

Education: Bachelor of Technology in Nautical Sciences, a Diploma from the Canadian Coast Guard College, and commercial certification as a Deck Officer (45-month program)

Interests: Engineering, physics, math, science

On an average day, Canadian Coast Guard employees will assist people in search and rescue cases, save lives, provide education on boating safety, and escort commercial ships through the ice. They will work on vessels anywhere in Canada.

The Canadian Coast Guard has three rescue centres across Canada.

Scientists use data storage tags to monitor Atlantic salmon populations.

Scientist with the Department of Fisheries and Oceans Canada

Duties: Scientists make significant contributions to research, development, and understanding of Canada's bodies of water, which includes its bordering three oceans, freshwater areas, and coastlines

Education: Master's or doctorate degree

Interests: Biology, math, physics

A scientist may specialize in one of five areas of research.

Hydrography, which is the study of water levels and tides, provides important nautical charts for people in the recreational and commercial fishing industries.

Fisheries research looks at how to conserve Canadian fishery resources so we can sustain them for the longest period of time.

Environmental scientists study the physical, chemical and biological conditions that affect the aquatic environment in which marine life live.

Ocean scientists are interested in physical and biological research of the oceans on Canada's coastlines. They want to better understand the ecosystems by conducting ocean-climate studies. Aquaculture scientists conduct research on the latest trends and technologies in the rapidly growing aquaculture industry.

Facing the Issues

The fishing industry is essential and vastly important to the Canadian economy. Fishing has long been important to the character of the Atlantic provinces, but the industry has been in decline in recent times due mostly to over-fishing the ocean for many years.

Conservation in the fishing industry was already a key issue in the early 1990s when stocks of cod had become so low that a ban on fishing them was enforced. Cod is still scarce, and there is still no commercial cod fishery off Newfoundland after almost 10 years of control.

Since then, the government has been far more active in the need to conserve fish stocks and has kept a tight control on how much fishing can take place. Canada was one of the first countries in the world to protect fish stocks and the aquatic environment by developing its own code of conduct for its domestic fisheries.

Salmon is by far Canada's most important species of farmed fish.

There has been a decrease in fish and sea products in Canada for many years, on both the east and west coasts. Fish reserves are still continuing to decline, but measures have now been put in place to make sure that future generations might still be in a position to consume sea products.

Until about 10 years ago, groundfish represented the largest volume of fish caught in the Canadian fishing industry. Fish such as redfish, flounder, pollock, and haddock have now fallen from the highest catch to the lowest, while the volume of shellfish has risen from the lowest to the highest. Shellfish catches are usually worth more per pound than other species, and this has encouraged an increase in the

Lobster is the most valuable shellfish caught in Canada.

The Canadian Food Inspection Agency has strict guidelines to make sure seafood is safe to be sold.

number of aquaculture businesses involved in their production. Salmon is by far Canada's most important species of farmed fish. Sales of salmon make up more than 80 percent of the value of the aquaculture industry in Canada.

Salmon population levels are of concern in the Atlantic and in some parts of the Pacific, but in northern British Columbia and Alaska, stocks are still abundant. The Skeena River alone has millions of wild salmon returning, which support commercial fisheries, Aboriginal food fisheries, and sports fisheries on the coast and around communities hundreds of miles inland.

The growth of fish farming in Canada has helped to maintain local economies in rural and coastal areas that were suffering from the decline in fishing stocks. Employment and business opportunities in servicing the aquaculture industry in these areas have grown. The manufacture of supplies, such as cages, nets, feed, and processing equipment, has added significantly to the work prospects of a wide range of young people with all sorts of skills and abilities.

Debate

With the decline of fish stocks in the oceans that surround eastern and western Canada, many people have left the fishing industry because they can no longer make a living. The aquaculture industry continues to grow, and many new jobs are being created. Is there a future in the fishing industry for young people?

YES Even with declining stocks, the capture fishery still accounts for 76 percent of total fish and seafood production in Canada.

By 2030, the aquaculture industry will become the dominant supplier of seafood and fish in Canada. Many new jobs are being created every year.

It is estimated that the aquaculture industry will continue to grow at a high rate until 2030 before levelling off.

NO Employment will continue to decline due to the depletion of fish stocks and the restrictions in both commercial and recreational fishing.

Work in the fishing industry is not attractive as it is strenuous and hazardous, and a steady year-round income cannot be guaranteed.

Although the aquaculture industry continues to grow, increased use of technology will reduce the number of people employed.

Fishing in the World

The world's fishing industry is diverse. At one extreme are large, multinational joint ventures that use huge factory trawlers and numerous other vessels, and employ thousands of workers on several oceans. At the other extreme, small boats are used by individual fishers who catch sufficient food for their families and sell any left over in their local communities. Most fishing operations fall somewhere between these extremes.

As the global population is expected to increase by 36 percent to 8.3 billion people in 2030, it is estimated that the annual demand for seafood will be 183 million tonnes. It is predicted that world supplies of fish and seafood will be only between 150 to 160 million tonnes—a shortfall of around 25 million tonnes each year.

Meeting the annual demand on a sustainable basis will be difficult, as global fisheries will only be able to provide 80 to 100 million tonnes per year. Aquaculture is destined to become an important additional source for the supply of fish and seafood as the ocean stocks continue to

The world aquaculture industry is growing faster than any other animal food producing industry.

Traditional fishers in Seychelles often use open boats and nets when fishing close to shore.

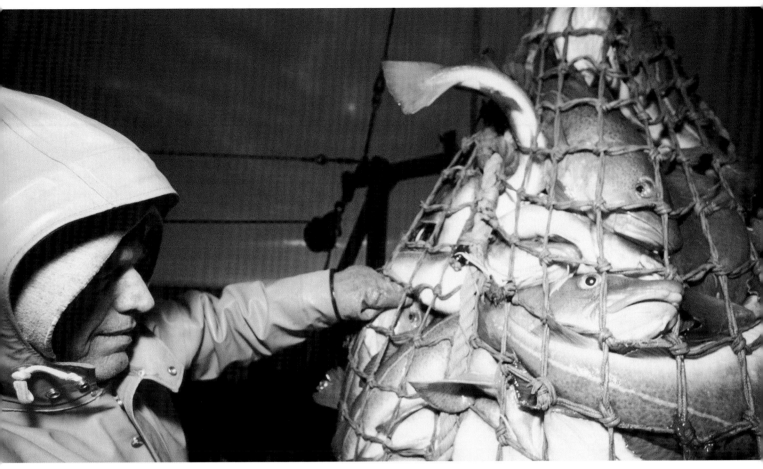

decline. By 2030, the aquaculture industry will supply almost half of the fish and seafood consumed around the world.

The world aquaculture industry is growing faster than any other animal-food producing industry. Aquaculture in China has increased hugely in recent years, and now produces more than 70 percent of the total volume of farmed fish and shellfish in the world. Meanwhile, Canada's aquaculture industry has increased in size at an annual rate of 20 percent every year for the past 20 years.

Canada has a worldwide reputation for supplying high quality fish and shellfish. Canadian salmon is now exported to more than 130 countries and is an important factor in our economy.

There are many different species of cod around the world.

BUSINESS BITS

Canada has one of the major commercial fishing industries in the world, exporting more than 75 percent of its fish and seafood production. Canada is now the world's fifth-largest exporter of fish and seafood products, with exports to more than 130 countries, with the United States being the largest customer.

China and Peru are the top fish and seafood producing countries followed by Japan, the United States, Chile, Indonesia, the Russian Federation, and India.

The world's largest volume of fish is caught in the northwestern Pacific, particularly the Bering Sea and the Sea of Japan. More than a quarter of the world's catch comes from this area.

Fishing Around the World

Fishing is an important industry throughout the world. People are increasingly farming the ocean as much as they farm the land. More than one species of fish is often harvested from a particular area. Commercial fishing may take place in a small lake, a river, or it may extend across an enormous area of an ocean. Fishing fleets from major countries across the world travel vast distances to gather fish from their breeding grounds.

THINK ABOUT IT

This map shows the ranges of some of the major fish catches. Where are Atlantic cod usually caught, and why do they live there?

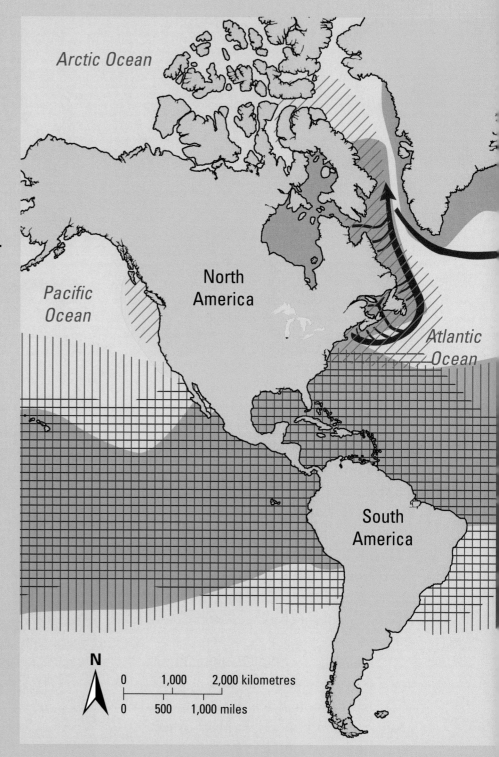

Arctic Ocean

Pacific Ocean

North America

Atlantic Ocean

South America

N

| 0 | 1,000 | 2,000 kilometres |

| 0 | 500 | 1,000 miles |

Northern Shrimp

Southern Bluefin Tuna

Yellowfin Tuna

Albacore Tuna

Skipjack Tuna

Atlantic Cod

Atlantic Salmon

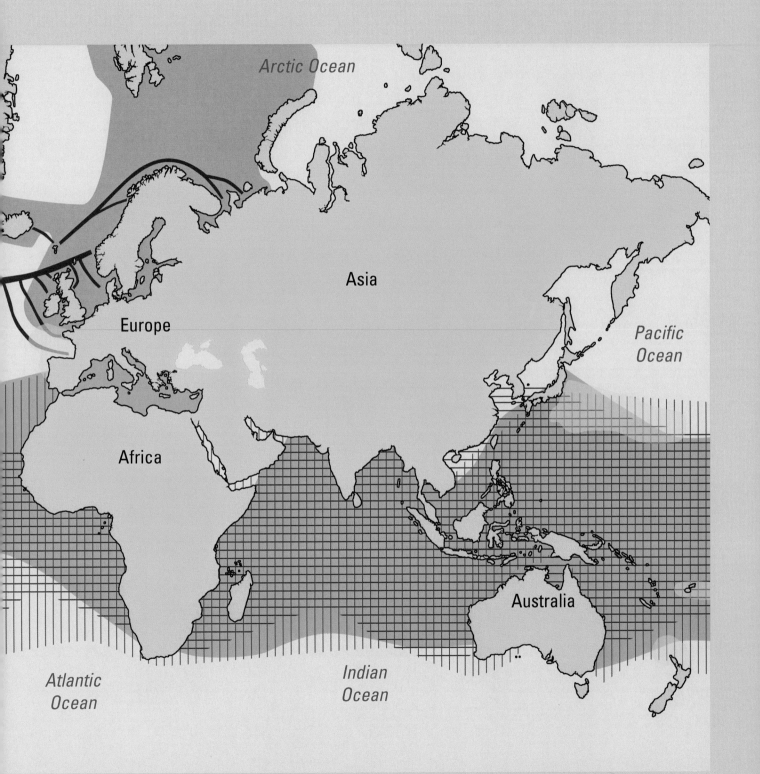

Arctic Ocean

Asia

Europe

Pacific
Ocean

Africa

Australia

Atlantic
Ocean

Indian
Ocean

Charting Fishing in the World

Total Fishing Production in the World

The world's oceans, lakes, and rivers are rich in fish and seafood resources. This chart shows how different areas rank in today's fishing industry. Production figures represent all sea fishing, freshwater fishing, and aquaculture.

2003 (million tonnes)

Far East	770,619,240
Asia	83,714,990
Central America & Caribbean	15,953,216
Europe	13,101,400
North America	6,713,210
Middle East & North Africa	3,601,189
Oceania	1,324,910

Major Fishing Countries of the World

Water covers more than 70 percent of Earth's surface. Different regions in the world are rich in various species, and fishing fleets from several countries will travel thousands of miles to fish in the most productive waters.

2003 (million tonnes)

China	47,297,750
Peru	6,103,478
USA	5,483,285
Japan	5,455,828
India	5,904,584
Indonesia	5,671,759
Russian Federation	3,389,932

Cod, Haddock, and Hake Fished in Atlantic and Arctic Waters
1997 - 2003

The waters off the coast of Newfoundland are among the most famous cod fishing areas in the world. Since the moratorium on cod fishing was imposed in 1992, stocks are beginning to show signs of improvement, and a limited amount of commercial fishing is now taking place.

(million tonnes)

Year	Value
2003	63
2002	9
2001	6
2000	3
1999	10
1998	18
1997	21

Salmon Caught by Canadian Fishers in the Atlantic Ocean
1997 – 2003

Atlantic salmon is fished in the north Atlantic as far north as the Arctic Circle. Atlantic salmon provides about 8 to 15 percent of the total world salmon catch. Salmon are among the most valuable fish caught, and they are used almost exclusively for human consumption.

(million tonnes)

Year	Value
2003	35,521
2002	42,455
2001	37,948
2000	34,211
1999	23,593
1998	17,715
1997	21,646

Supplying the Demand

In the fishing industry, prices are dictated by the rules of supply and demand. Lobsters, as well as tuna, were once regarded as the poor man's food and nowhere near the delicacies they are considered today. Lobsters were once so plentiful at the turn of the 19th century that they were used by early settlers to fertilize their fields.

Over-fishing had brought the oyster to near-extinction in Prince Edward Island by 1910. Its value had increased accordingly, seeing prices rise from $1 a barrel when they were plentiful in the 1880s to $12 a barrel by 1920 when they were scarce. This

As a result of rising demand, the prices of most fresh and frozen fish have risen since World War II.

only encouraged more harvesting of the remaining oysters, and threatened to wipe out the stocks completely. The government had to pass legislation to protect and save the oyster stock. Today the oysters thrive again, and Prince Edward Island oysters are exported around the world.

The supplies of fish in the world's oceans once seemed inexhaustible. Not any more. In the past 30 years, the production and consumption of fish has risen so dramatically that the world's wild fisheries may fall victim to their own success.

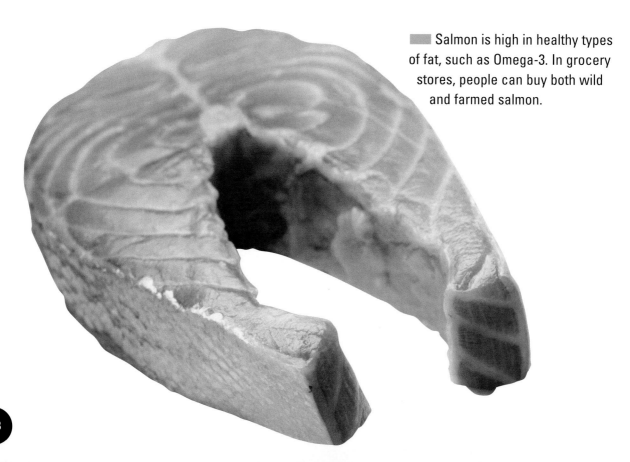

Salmon is high in healthy types of fat, such as Omega-3. In grocery stores, people can buy both wild and farmed salmon.

The consumption of fish worldwide has doubled since 1973, and the developing world has been responsible for nearly all of this growth.

Countries such as China and India, which are experiencing rapid increases in population and a fast growth in their economies, tend to have the greatest increases in consumption of all animal products, including fish. Consumption of seafood in the **developed countries** has dropped a little over the past few years.

Besides being used as food, fish is also in increased demand for use as feed. Nearly one-third of the world's wild-caught fish are "reduced" to fishmeal and fish oil, which are then used in feeds for livestock such as poultry and pigs, or for **fertilizers** used in agriculture.

As a result of rising demand, the prices of most fresh and frozen fish have risen since World War II. In contrast, the prices of most animal-origin foods have decreased steeply over the past several decades. Exceptions to the general rise in fish prices are canned finfish, which have declined in popularity in developed countries since the early 1970s, and some individual commodities, such as shrimp and salmon, which have seen huge gains in production thanks to aquaculture.

Although breeding technology in aquaculture is in its relative infancy, breeders have significantly raised production for some commercial species, such as salmon, trout, and **tilapia**. For the future, the successful cultivation and breeding of other species, such as cod and bluefin tuna, should be a tremendous boost to the supply of fish to the world.

BUSINESS BITS

British Columbia and New Brunswick are the two major aquaculture producers in Canada, followed by Prince Edward Island.

British Columbia is the fourth largest producer of farmed salmon in the world.

Aquaculture is the fastest growing sector of food production in the world.

Freshness in all foods is an important part of quality, and fish and seafood is delivered from the water to the consumer within days, often within 24 hours.

Commercial Value of Canadian Fishing Industry 1993 – 2003

Year	Value in thousand dollars
1993	1,483,585
1994	1,768,126
1995	1,860,693
1996	1,634,891
1997	1,704,789
1998	1,684,777
1999	1,987,894
2000	2,220,919
2001	2,192,136
2002	2,214,313
2003	2,310,800

THINK ABOUT IT

The cost of Canadian salmon has decreased over the years. What are the possible reasons for this?

From Canada to the World

In 2005, Canada's fish and seafood exports reached $4.3 billion. Canada's largest export market is the United States (63 percent of seafood trade), followed by Japan (11 percent), and the European Union (9.9 percent). Significant annual trade surpluses have been created as a result of Canada's fish and seafood imports staying at around $2 billion.

Canada's aquaculture industry is responding to the demand for fish and seafood. Production has more than doubled during the past 10 years. More than 85 percent of Canada's farmed fish and seafood production is exported.

Nova Scotia is Canada's top exporter of fish and seafood products, with a value of $1.09 billion.

Successful marketing of aquaculture products depends on consumer confidence in product safety and quality. The federal and provincial governments ensure that the highest standards of product quality and safety are maintained.

The Canadian Food Inspection Agency has an export certification program that ensures Canadian seafood sold abroad will meet a level of standards acceptable to importing countries. Official documentation is provided so that buyers can make sure that the safety and freshness guidelines are met for international seafood markets.

Nova Scotia is Canada's top exporter of fish and seafood products with a value of

Much of the fishing industry in the United States occurs along the north Atlantic coast, in areas such as Boston, Massachusetts.

THINK ABOUT IT ▼

A large percentage of Canada's seafood trade is with the United States. Why is the United States such an important trading partner?

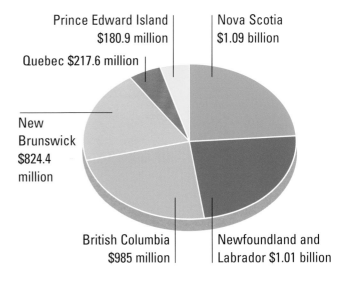

Farmed salmon are raised from eggs on hatcheries. Eggs from Canada are exported around the world.

$1.09 billion. The province exported 145,881 tonnes of seafood in 2004. Newfoundland and Labrador was the second most valuable exporter of fish and seafood with products valued at $1.01 billion.

Top Five Importers of Canadian Seafood (2005)
(tonnes)

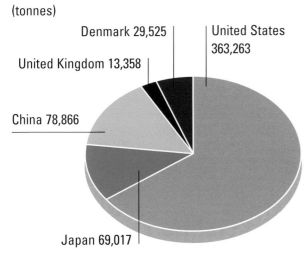

Denmark 29,525

United Kingdom 13,358

China 78,866

United States 363,263

Japan 69,017

Value of Seafood Exported by Provinces (2004)

Prince Edward Island $180.9 million

Quebec $217.6 million

New Brunswick $824.4 million

Nova Scotia $1.09 billion

British Columbia $985 million

Newfoundland and Labrador $1.01 billion

Fishing Science

The technological development and widespread use in the fishing industry of synthetic fibres, hydraulic equipment for gear and fish handling, electronics for fish finding, and satellite-based technology for navigation and communications have all contributed to the expansion of fisheries and aquaculture in recent decades. Technical advances have generally led to more efficient and economical fishing and a reduction of the physical labour required.

Trawling nets are made from polyethylene.

Developments in electronics, refrigeration, ice-making, and fish processing equipment have made it possible for large vessels to remain at sea and fish for months at a time.

In recent years, the introduction of modern materials have made changes in the design and size of some fishing nets possible. Modern commercial nets used for catching shrimps allow finfish to escape from them so that stocks of young fish are not wasted while fishing for shrimp. These nets have a square mesh window that allows fish to escape upwards through the large

Farmed fish eat food pellets that are similar to those fed to pet fish.

farmed. Providing additional food, adding seed fish collected elsewhere, and managing water systems to maintain adequate oxygen levels for the fish are all possible using modern technology. Major advances are being made in the technology of the production of **aquafeeds**, which combine a large number of ingredients into very small feed pellets to feed the fish stock. These developments help improve the growing conditions and the quality of farmed fish, and they also help to avoid the spread of disease in the stock.

Sea ranching, the release of young fish into the wild to improve the harvest in capture fisheries, has made a start but its long-term viability is still to be assessed.

The impact of such changes has considerably increased the earnings of the fishing industry, but it also underlines the need for effective control to prevent over-fishing. Recent technical innovation has been focussed on improving the ability of fishers to select different species of fish to help avoid over-fishing and to maintain existing stocks.

square mesh, while the shrimp that do not swim as well as fish pass into the net.

The electronics industry has rapidly developed new forms of **echosounders**, including **sonar**, to use on fishing vessels. Sonar detects objects underwater by using sound waves. Modern versions of sonar are able to electronically sweep the area of sea around the fishing vessel for signs of shoals of fish.

Much of the technology used in aquaculture is relatively simple, amounting to small modifications that improve the growth and survival rates of the particular species being

In recent years, the introduction of modern materials have made changes in the design and size of some fishing nets possible.

BUSINESS BITS

There are more than 3.5 million fishing vessels operating in the world's oceans.

A modern supertrawler can be longer than a football field and capable of catching and processing up to 200 tonnes of fish daily.

Eighty percent of the world's marine catch is produced by just 20 fishing nations.

Fishing's Impact on Canadians

The fishing industry supplies food for both humans and animals. It also provides around 130,000 jobs for Canadians. About half of these work directly as fishers, while the rest are employed in associated industries. More than half the fishers are self-employed. This is among the highest proportion in the Canadian workforce. Fishing is a major export industry in the Canadian economy and is therefore very important to the nation. Over-fishing and environmental problems, however, are a threat to the successful future of the industry.

Fishing can be a difficult and hazardous occupation. Life as a fisherman involves strenuous outdoor work and long hours.

Recreational fishing is a popular pastime for Canadians.

Fishers sell their catch to various customers. Many sell directly to the customer in fish markets, while others sell to grocery stores and restaurants. In recent years, there has been a significant growth of fishers selling their fish and seafood directly to consumers through the internet. Food processing plants are also supplied by the commercial fishing industry.

Fishing employees more than 7,000 fishermen and 5,000 plant workers in New Brunswick, while aquaculture creates about 4,000 jobs.

The Canadian fishing industry generates about five billion dollars a year.

Commercial fishing is the mainstay to the economy of about 1,500 communities in rural and coastal Canada. Many aquaculture operations are located in these communities, and they provide new jobs at a time when other traditional fishing businesses are experiencing a downturn.

Recreational fishing is a popular pastime for Canadians. Anglers spend around $4.7 billion a year on fishing trips for food, accommodation, transportation, fishing supplies, and other services related to the sport.

The fishing industry has to ensure that the products it sells are safe and of good quality so that people continue to want to buy it. Farmed Canadian salmon, for example, has an excellent worldwide reputation. This reputation is protected by good fishing methods and safe **husbandry**. Many livelihoods depend upon it. Fishers and scientists are continually working together to make sure that stocks of fish and seafood are sustainable for future generations, safe, and of good quality

Care of the supplies of fish and seafood from Canadian waters is an essential part of the industry. The Canadian Food Inspection Agency is one of the world's most respected fish inspection and control systems. The agency provides exporters with official documentation that Canadian fish and seafood products meet the increasingly thorough standards required by the world's major seafood markets.

BUSINESS BITS

Aquaculture provides sustainable, year-round employment for more than 47,000 people living in coastal and rural communities. There are aquaculture businesses in 16 Aboriginal communities, which provide stable employment and resources for their communities.

Scientists continue to work on ways to reduce health risks associated with the use of pesticides in aquaculture. New methods to reduce the use of pesticides through pest management and other environmentally friendly techniques help to protect consumers.

Helping Others

Fishing is an important industry worldwide for the supply of food. Canada's fisheries have provided for Canadians and people all over the world for centuries. Because the waters surrounding Canada's coast have become over-fished by vessels from other countries, there has had to be a reduction in the amount of fishing allowed in these waters so that fish stocks and their environment can replenish. This process takes many years and has to be monitored carefully.

Canada helps these countries through many projects run by the Canadian International Development Agency (CIDA).

People from countries such as Eritrea have come to Nova Scotia to learn about lobster fishing.

Canada has skilled workers who have the knowledge to improve fishing methods and to create sustainable fishing businesses. Many underdeveloped nations do not have this expertise and are often too poor to buy the stock and equipment necessary to create aquaculture. Canada helps these countries through many projects run by the Canadian International Development Agency (CIDA).

CIDA works in partnership with developing countries, Canadian organizations, institutions, and businesses, as well as international organizations and agencies. The goal for the agency in most cases is to show people how to look after their fish stocks and to create

environments in which they can safely farm fish. Canada provides funding for programs and equipment, as well as experts who help develop fishing techniques suitable to their waters. Once these new fishing enterprises are up and running, CIDA helps further by giving advice about selling the products in national and international markets.

While **high-tech technology** is available to the large fishing fleets and aquaculture of the developed world, technology in many small-scale fisheries in underdeveloped countries may amount to no more than motorizing a dugout canoe, the use of modern and lighter gear, or using iceboxes to ensure the quality of the fish landed.

Oxfam Canada is part of an international development agency that works with partners around the world on developing sustainable communities. As part of this program, community workers from Eritrea have attended Nova Scotia's International Institute in Antigonish and have spent some time visiting with eastern Canadian communities that are involved in inshore fishing. Both men and women have received the equipment, and vocational and management training they need to support the fishing industry to prevent fish stocks in Eritrea from completely disappearing.

Tsunami Relief

Oxfam has played an important role in helping the residents of Sri Lanka and Thailand regain their livelihoods after the **tsunami** of 2004 wiped out the fishing communities. It provided boats, equipment, and cash assistance to help the surviving men and women get back up on their feet again.

The fishing industry in Sri Lanka is gradually moving towards returning to pre-tsunami conditions. The Sri Lankan government estimates that 15,300 boats were destroyed, but that 12,900 replacements have been pledged by donors. A further 4,592 boats that were damaged have been repaired and are once more seaworthy. By August 2005, the fish catch had recovered to nearly 70 percent of the previous year's amount, having previously fallen by 95 percent in January 2005.

McMaster University in Hamilton, Ontario, responded to the plight of fishing communities in the northeast region of Sri Lanka through Relief Aid International. They secured the help of boat builders from Great Britain who had developed new technology to make resin injection moulded boats. This project helped bring modern technology and practical relief to the area.

Students from the university went to Sri Lanka to help local people plan the building of a boat factory in the Kinniya region, which is equipped with the new production equipment. New fishing boats are now being made, and traditional boat designs are also being recreated using the new technology provided.

Looking to the Future

The Canadian fishing industry faces a challenging future. One of the key challenges is the current depletion of fish stocks. Canada is one of the first countries in the world to protect fish stocks and the aquatic environment by developing its own code of conduct for its domestic fisheries.

The fishing industry has learned from past mistakes and is preparing for a productive future. A fundamental change in the way fisheries are managed and operated is essential to recover fish stocks and create healthy fisheries and newly developed commercial fisheries.

Science plays an important role in Canada's strategy to combat over-fishing and improve international fisheries. Sound fisheries management is based on sound science. Science and technology are providing the fishing industry with improved information and new equipment that makes the industry more efficient and less wasteful of its natural resources. Commercial fishing vessels are increasingly being fitted with new electronic technology

The growth in aquaculture is vital to a successful future for the fishing industry.

that helps improve navigation and fish detection. The effects of increased automation and technology will have to be monitored carefully to avoid repeating the mistakes of over-fishing in previous years.

The growth in aquaculture is a vital to a successful future for the fishing industry. Twenty-five percent of all the seafood that is consumed worldwide is grown in fish farms. This figure is sure to rise as the population and demand increases.

The success of aquaculture with species like salmon and shrimp has been huge, but if we want to see further expansions, there will have to be more use made of **by-products**. The waste, for example, that is produced by the salmon farms can be the source of nutrients for further growing of seaweeds. Seaweeds are an important product used in the food, cosmetic, and pharmaceutical industries.

Scallops are one of the marine species that can be successfully farmed in Canada.

In the future, we will see much more integration of the different aquaculture activities, in which, for example, salmon, seaweed, and mussels are all be grown alongside each other. This is called **polyculture**. Experiments have shown that within a certain distance from the salmon cages, seaweeds grow significantly faster than those that were located farther offshore. Mussels can benefit from the micro algae that will bloom as a result of nutrients directly and indirectly released at the salmon farm.

In freshwater aquaculture, there will also be more integration with other farming practices, called **aquaponics**. The same water that is used in an aquaculture farm can also be used later on agricultural land. This water is loaded with nutrients such as nitrogen and phosphorous, nutrients that are vital components in fertilizers for agriculture.

Although the methods used in aquaponics have been practised for many

Fish can be turned into organic fertilizer to help plants grow.

years, the emergence of food production systems based on this science is a fairly new concept. It is a practice that is receiving considerable interest due to an ever-increasing need for fresh, wholesome food, and sustainable, eco-friendly agriculture practices.

Insider Viewpoint

What does the future hold for Canada's fishing industry? Take a look at what people working inside the industry think.

"…there's a big future for fish and fisheries out there. Most of these stocks will recover and they'll recover with a bunch of people chasing them that understand that you can screw up. One of our best fisheries here in Canada is the Pacific herring fishery. We drove the herring stocks in the 60's down to maybe two percent of what they were shipping. That thing's bounced back, it's enormously valuable, and there's nobody involved in that industry that wants to do anything stupid again…"

Carl Walters, professor at the Fishery Centre at the University of British Columbia

"…awareness is only the first step. We need to act. This can happen at all levels, from a local beach clean-up campaign to regional cooperation in coastal management or global data-sharing on climate change. Finding ways to bring together municipal departments responsible for tourism, for construction, for sewage treatment, aquaculture and forestry, would already be a massive step towards more sustainable coastal management."

Federico Mayor, Director-General of UNESCO

Timeline of Fishing Events

1534

Jacques Cartier comes to explore the Gulf of the St. Lawrence River.

1600

The Basques from Spain and France set up temporary settlements to fish the waters on Canada's east coast.

1603

Samuel de Champlain begins his explorations of the Maritime region.

1670

The charter of the Hudson's Bay Trading Company is granted to a group of English investors. The charter gives the company a fur, fish, and mining monopoly.

1821

The Hudson's Bay Company merges with arch the Montreal-based North West Company.

1825

The Erie Canal opens.

1845

The first lighthouse on Prince Edward Island is built at Point Prim.

1852

The Hudson's Bay Company begins to fish commercially.

1854

The Reciprocity Treaty is signed between the United States and Great Britain, eliminating fishing limits and allowing for free trade between **British North America** and the United States.

1867

The nation of Canada is created by the signing of Confederation.

1877

A Pacific herring catch is recorded for the first time.

1889

Fishing seasons are established to protect lobsters as they spawn.

1914-1918

World War I takes place.

1924

The first fisherman's union is created in Canada by Tignish fishermen.

1927

The first shipment of live lobsters to the United States market by Tignish Fisheries Limited occurs.

1929-1939

The Great Depression takes place.

1928

The United Maritime Fishermen (UMF) is formed.

1939-1945

World War II takes place.

1958

The St. Lawrence Seaway opens.

1965

Groundfish landings in Northwest Atlantic peak at 2.8 million tonnes.

1970s

Aquaculture begins on the coast of British Columbia. Fish farmers grow Atlantic and Pacific salmon.

1972

The commercial Pacific herring roe fishery begins.

1973

The first Global Positioning System is developed for navigational purposes.

1976

Canada announces a 200-nautical-mile coastal fishing zone.

1987

Canada bans the commercial hunt for whitecoats and bluebacks.

1992

Atlantic Canada's cod fishing industry is shut down due to over-fishing.

1993

All Canadian cod fishing is banned.

2001

The Columbia River salmon run was the greatest ever recorded since counts began in 1938.

2003

A $50 million action plan is developed to assist fishers, plant workers, and communities affected by the closure of three cod fisheries in Canadian waters.

2005

The United Nations Food and Agriculture Organization begins to collect information on deep-sea fish stocks and fishing activities in order to assess impacts on deep sea fish and ecosystems.

Research Activity

Jobs and More

Fishing benefits Canada in many ways. The fishing industry provides jobs for many Canadians, and the industry produces fish and seafood in various ways that people want to buy.

Fish is an important part of a healthy diet because of its high-quality protein content and generally low-fat content, and as a good source of **omega-3**, which is thought to have health benefits in all stages of life.

Make a list of all the fish products you normally eat. Now, choose one product that uses fish or seafood from Canadian waters that you would like to learn more about. (Hint: some fish products manufactured in Canada have a "Made in Canada" sticker on them.) Research the product, and try to answer the following questions. Report on your findings.

1. How many people does it take to make this product?
2. Who uses this product the most?
3. Where is the product made? Why is made there?
4. How is the environment affected when this product is made?
5. What issues does this type of fishing face?
6. How will this type of fishing change in the next 10 years?

Fish Recipe

Baked Salmon with Dill

Try making this fun and simple recipe.

Ingredients:

0.7 kg salmon steaks or skinless fillets
5 mL   dill weed
2.5 mL onion salt
1   lemon, sliced

Directions:

1. Preheat the oven to 210 degrees Celsius. Spray the baking dish with cooking oil. Place salmon in the dish.
2. Sprinkle with dill and onion salt, and top with lemon slices. Cover and bake for 15 to 20 minutes until flesh turns **opaque**.
3. Serve with extra lemon. Makes four servings.

What Do You Know?

M i X and Match

1. world's largest producer of seafood
2. the fourth largest producer of farmed
3. sell goods to other countries
4. an echosounder
5. main importer of Canadian fish
6. the number of fishing vessels in the
7. the farming of fish and seafoods
8. French sailor and explorer
9. breed of fish bred in aquaculture
10. industrialized countries
11. Canada's most important species of farmed fish

a) tilapia
b) the United States
c) aquaculture
d) salmon
e) China
f) 3.5 million
g) export
h) developed countries
i) sonar
j) Jacques Cartier
k) British Columbia

Answers: 1. e) 2. k) 3. g) 4. i) 5. b) 6. f) 7. c) 8. j) 9. a) 10. h) 11. d)

TRUE or FALSE?

1 Canada has the longest coastline in the world.

2 British Columbia is the fourth largest producer of farmed salmon in the world.

3 World aquaculture production is expected to exceed beef production in 2010.

4 Canada has the largest freshwater system in the world.

5 Hydrograhy is the study of high mountains.

6 Canadian salmon is exported to more than 130 countries.

Answers:
1. True 2. True
3. True 4. True
5. False 6. True

MULTIPLE Choice

1 **Which countries are the main customers for Canadian fishing?**

a) France, Japan, the United States, and the European Union

b) China, the United States, India, and Peru

c) The United States, Japan, the European Union, and China

d) India, France, the United States, and China

2 **Which are the main Canadian provinces for aquaculture?**

a) British Columbia, New Brunswick, and Prince Edward Island

b) Prince Edward Island, British Columbia, and Newfoundland

c) British Columbia, New Brunswick, and Newfoundland

d) Prince Edward Island, British Columbia, and Nova Scotia

3 **Where in the world is the largest volume of fish caught?**

a) The Atlantic Ocean

b) The Mediterranean Sea

c) The Pacific Ocean

d) The Indian Ocean

4 **Which is the major fishing country in the world?**

a) The United States

b) Japan

c) Canada

d) China

5 **Which province is the largest exporter of fish and seafood products?**

a) British Columbia

b) Prince Edward Island

c) Nova Scotia

d) Newfoundland

6 **About how many Canadian jobs are involved with the fishing industry?**

a) 500,00

b) 130,000

c) 1 million

d) 250,000

Answers:
1. c 2. a 3. c 4. d
5. c 6. b

45

Further Research

Books

These books provide more information on topics relating to Canadian fishing.

McMillan, Bruce. *Salmon Summer*. Boston: Walter Lorraine, 1998.

Winters, Adam. *Choosing a Career in the Fishing Industry*. New York: Rosen Publishing Group, 2001.

Websites

To find out more about Canadian fishing, check out these websites.

Fisheries and Oceans Canada
www.dfo-mpo.gc.ca

Canadian Aquaculture Industry Alliance
www.aquaculture.ca

Fish and Seafood Online
www.ats.agr.gc.ca/seafood/home-e.htm

The Canadian Encyclopedia
www.thecanadianencyclopedia.com

Glossary

aquafeeds: feed that is manufactured to feed farmed fish and seafood a carefully balanced diet, usually made in pellet form

aquaponics: growing plants and fish together in the same controlled system

British North America: what are now the provinces of Ontario, Quebec, Nova Scotia, and New Brunswick

by-products: secondary products that occur as a result of manufacturing something else

developed countries: countries that have undergone the process of industrialization

echosounders: sounding apparatus used to determine the depth of sea beneath a ship or boat

expertise: skill or judgment through knowledge

exports: sends goods to another country for sale

fertilizers: substances put on the land to make it able to produce more crops

Great Depression: an economic crisis that took place during the 1930s

high-tech technology: advanced technological development

husbandry: the management of resources

industrialization: the development of large industries as a feature of an economic system

markets: places where items can be sold

moratorium: a temporary suspension of an activity

omega-3: polyunsaturated fatty acids found in oil from fish and certain plant oils

opaque: not penetrated by light

polyculture: stocking two or more complementary species in the same water

rural: in the country instead of in the city

scurvy: a disease caused by a lack of vitamin C

sextant: an instrument used in navigation

sonar: a system of detecting fish or objects under the water by using reflected sound waves

supertrawlers: huge fishing trawlers more than 140 metres long with massive freezing and storage facilities

sustainable: able to support for a long period of time

tilapia: also known widely as St. Peter's fish, a spiny-finned, freshwater fish native chiefly to Africa and the Middle East

tsunami: a series of huge waves generated when a body of water, such as a lake or ocean, is rapidly displaced on a massive scale, usually caused by undersea earthquakes. The effects of a tsunami can range from unnoticeable to devastating.

Index

aquaculture 7, 14, 18, 19, 21, 22, 23, 26, 29, 30, 32, 33, 34, 35, 36, 37, 38, 39, 41, 44, 45, 46

aquaponics 39

British Columbia 14, 21, 29, 31, 39, 41, 44, 45

Canadian Food Inspection Agency 21, 30, 35

Canadian International Development Agency (CIDA) 36

Cartier, Jacques 10, 11, 15, 40, 44

echosounder 33, 44

fertilizer 29, 39

fishing production 26, 30

Labrador 11, 15, 31

lobster 4, 7,8, 16, 20, 28, 36, 40, 41

mussels 14, 39

Newfoundland 10, 11, 15, 20, 27, 31, 40, 45

Nova Scotia 30, 31, 37, 45

omega-3 28, 42

Oxfam 15, 37

oyster 14, 28

Prince Edward Island 11, 14, 28, 29, 31, 40, 45

recreational fishing 6, 8, 21, 35

refrigeration 11, 32

satellite 32

seaweed 38, 39

sonar 33, 44

tilapia 29, 44

tsunami 37

tuna 24, 28, 29